HOW TO DRAW
EXTREME
SPORTS

David Antram

PowerKiDS
press™

New York

Published in 2012 by The Rosen Publishing Group, Inc.
29 East 21st Street, New York, NY 10010

Editor: Rob Walker
U.S. Editor: Kara Murray

Library of Congress Cataloging-in-Publication Data

Antram, David, 1958-
 Extreme sports / by David Antram. — 1st ed.
     p. cm. — (How to draw)
 Includes index.
 ISBN 978-1-4488-6459-1 (library binding) — ISBN 978-1-4488-6465-2 (pbk.) —
ISBN 978-1-4488-6466-9 (6-pack)
1. Sports in art—Juvenile literature. 2. Athletes in art—Juvenile literature.
3. Extreme sports—Juvenile literature.
4. Drawing—Technique—Juvenile literature. I. Title. II. Series.
NC825.S62A58 2012
743'.89796—dc22

2011017639

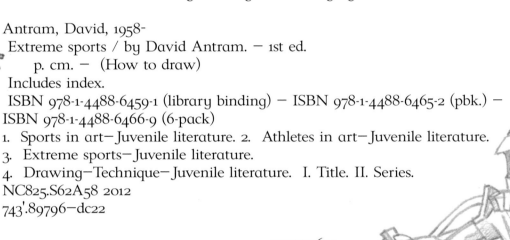

Manufactured in Heshan, China

CPSIA Compliance Information: Batch #SW2102PK:
For Further Information contact Rosen Publishing,
New York, New York at 1-800-237-9932

PAPER FROM
SUSTAINABLE
FORESTS

Contents

Making a Start

Learning to draw is about looking and seeing. Keep practicing and get to know your subject. Use a sketchbook to make quick sketches. Start by doodling and experimenting with shapes and patterns. There are many ways to draw. This book shows one method. Visit art galleries, look at artists' drawings, see how friends draw, but above all, find your own way.

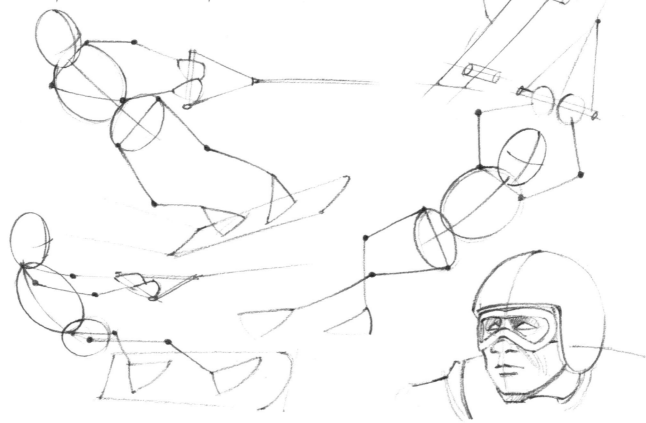

Use simple shapes to draw the figures in action with their equipment.

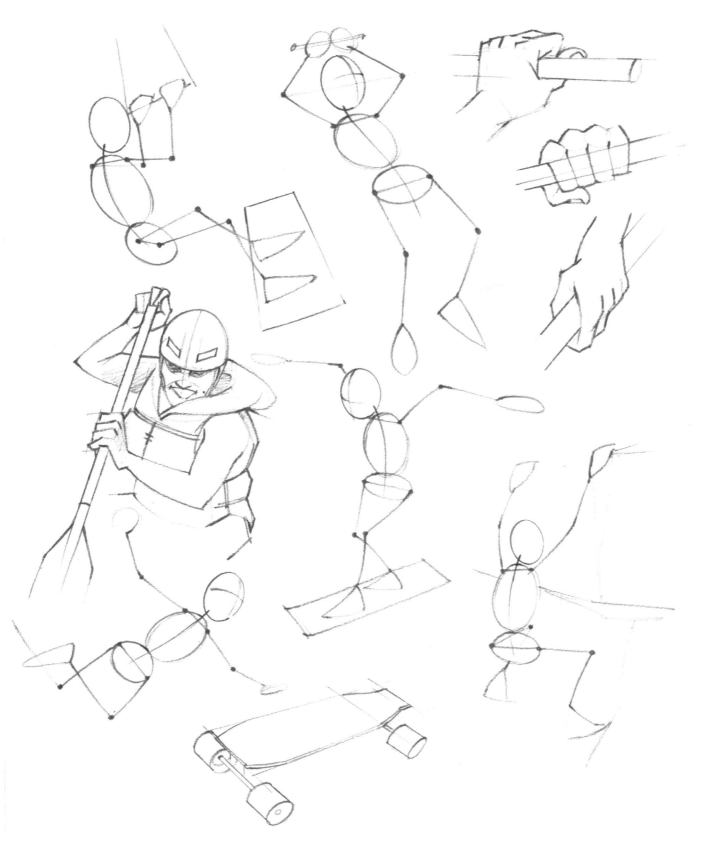

Perspective

If you look at any object from different viewpoints, you will see that the part that is closest to you looks larger, and the part farthest away from you looks smaller. Drawing in perspective is a way of creating a feeling of space, or of showing three dimensions on a flat surface.

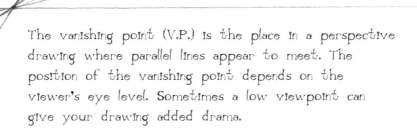

V.P.

V.P.

The vanishing point (V.P.) is the place in a perspective drawing where parallel lines appear to meet. The position of the vanishing point depends on the viewer's eye level. Sometimes a low viewpoint can give your drawing added drama.

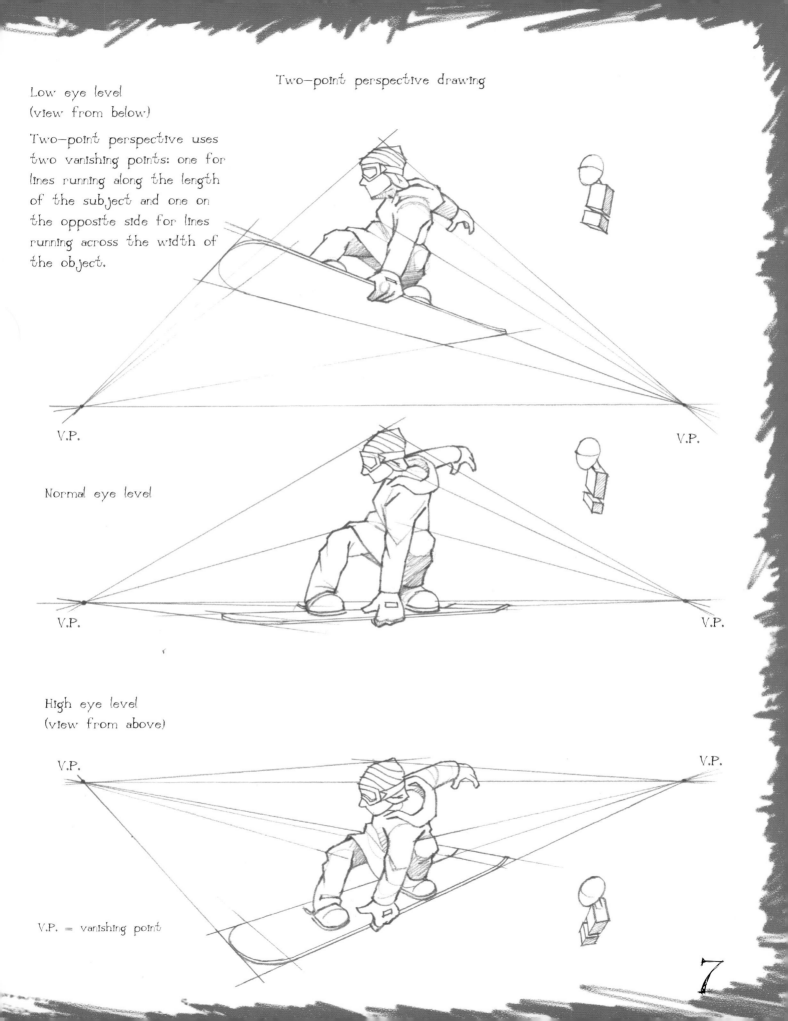

Low eye level
(view from below)

Two-point perspective uses
two vanishing points: one for
lines running along the length
of the subject and one on
the opposite side for lines
running across the width of
the object.

V.P.   V.P.

Normal eye level

V.P.   V.P.

High eye level
(view from above)

V.P.   V.P.

V.P. = vanishing point

7

Drawing Tools

Here are just a few of the many tools that you can use for drawing. Let your imagination go, and have fun experimenting with all the different marks you can make.

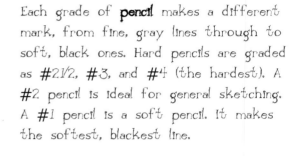

Pencil

Watercolor pencil

Charcoal pencil

Charcoal stick

Pastels

Finger painting

Black, gray, and white pastel on gray construction paper

Each grade of **pencil** makes a different mark, from fine, gray lines through to soft, black ones. Hard pencils are graded as #2½, #3, and #4 (the hardest). A #2 pencil is ideal for general sketching. A #1 pencil is a soft pencil. It makes the softest, blackest line.

Watercolor pencils come in many different colors and make a line similar to a #2 pencil. Paint over your finished drawing with clean water, though, and the lines will soften and run.

It is less messy and easier to achieve a fine line with a **charcoal pencil** than a stick of charcoal. Create soft tones by smudging lines with your finger. **Ask an adult** to spray the drawing with fixative to prevent further smudging.

Pastels are brittle sticks of powdered color. They blend and smudge easily and are ideal for quick sketches. Pastel drawings work well on textured, colored paper. **Ask an adult** to spray your finished drawing with fixative.

Experiment with **finger painting**. Your fingerprints make exciting patterns and textures. Use your fingers to smudge soft pencil, charcoal, and pastel lines.

Ballpoint pens are very useful for sketching and making notes. Make different tones by building up layers of shading.

A **mapping pen** has to be dipped into bottled ink to fill the nib. Different nib shapes make different marks. Try putting a diluted ink wash over parts of the finished drawing.

Draftsmen's pens and specialist **art pens** can produce extremely fine lines and are ideal for creating surface texture.
A variety of pen nibs are available that produce different widths of line.

Felt-tip pens are ideal for quick sketches. If the ink is not waterproof, try drawing on wet paper and see what happens.

Broad-nibbed **marker pens** make interesting lines and are good for large, bold sketches. Try using a black pen for the main sketch and a gray one to block in areas of shadow.

Paintbrushes are shaped differently to make different marks. Japanese brushes are soft and produce beautiful, flowing lines. Large sable brushes are good for painting a wash over a line drawing. Fine brushes are good for drawing delicate lines.

Ballpoint pen

Mapping pen

Draftsman's pen

Felt-tip pen

Marker pen

Paintbrush

Materials

Try using different types of drawing papers and materials. Experiment with charcoal, wax crayons, and pastels. All pens, from felt-tips to ballpoints, will make interesting marks. Try drawing with pen and ink on wet paper.

Ink silhouette

Silhouette is a style of drawing that mainly uses solid black shapes.

Felt-tips come in a range of line widths. The wider pens are good for filling in large areas of flat tone.

Remember, the best equipment
and materials will not
necessarily make the best
drawing. Only practice will!

Pencil drawings can include a
vast amount of detail and tone.
Try experimenting with the
different grades of pencil to get
a range of light and shade
effects in your drawing.

Hatching

Lines drawn in **ink** cannot be erased, so keep
your ink drawings sketchy and less rigid. Don't
worry about mistakes, as these can be lost in
the drawing as it develops.

It can be tricky adding light and shade to
a drawing with a pen. Use a solid layer
of ink for the very darkest
areas and
cross—hatching
(straight lines
criss—crossing each
other) for ordinary
dark tones. Hatching (straight
lines running parallel to each other)
can be used for midrange tones.

Cross—hatching

Wheels

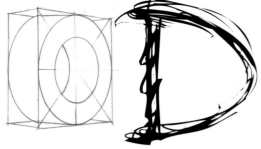

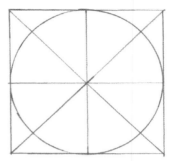

Fit the circle in the box.

Drawing wheels from different perspectives can be tricky. The solution is to use construction lines to draw a square or perspective box, then fit the wheel within it.

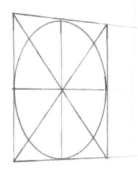

As the square turns into a perspective viewpoint, the circle becomes an ellipse.

First draw a perspective box with vertical and horizontal lines running through the center. Draw in the perimeter of the wheel, paying attention to the construction lines to make sure it touches at the edges of the perspective box, at the top, bottom, left, and right. Add an inner ellipse for the inside of the wheel.

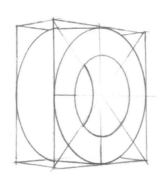

Examples of different perspective wheels and the construction boxes needed

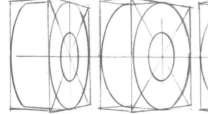 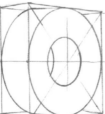 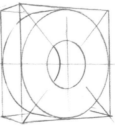 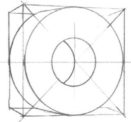 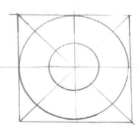

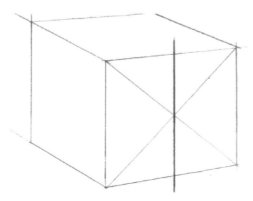

How to find the center point.

To find the center point of the perspective box, simply draw two lines from corner to corner. The point where they cross is the center. Use this point to add your center lines.

Perspective boxes

When you create your perspective boxes for the wheels, remember to consider the vanishing point of the object to which they are attached.

In this drawing the skateboard has a completely different vanishing point from the figure because it is at a different angle.

The perspective boxes for the wheels will use the same vanishing point you used for the structure of the skateboard.

V.P.

Dramatic Heights

The choice of background can often add tension and drama to drawings of extreme sports. Here are two sports seen from a great height. The use of perspective drawing in relation to the figure gives a great sense of height and danger.

The climber clings perilously to a rock face. Use perspective to show how steep the rock face is as it falls away into the distance.

Add shading to areas where the light wouldn't reach to help create a three-dimensional effect.

The parachutist falls to
a faraway airfield.

Use perspective to draw
the airfield in relation to
the falling parachutist.

Consider the scale of the
buildings to show how far
down the airfield is.

When your drawing is
complete, remove unwanted
construction lines.

15

Freestyle BMX

The BMX is the perfect bike for freestyling. With pegs attached and a flexible setup, riders are capable of performing amazing tricks and stunts.

Start by drawing the rider as a simple stick figure with dots to indicate joints.

Add ovals for the head, body, hips, and hands.

Draw simple triangles for the feet.

Using straight lines, mark out the frame of the BMX.

Using the construction lines as a guide, add tube shapes for the legs and circles for knees.

Sketch in the position of the facial features.

Using the construction lines as a guide, add tube shapes for the arms with circles for elbows.

Add more detail to the shape of the feet.

Add the BMX wheels to the bike frame.

Add parts of the frame and pegs.

Draw in the rider's T-shirt.

Add some hair and a cap.

Sketch in basic shapes for the hands and fingers.

Draw the wheels using construction lines to help with perspective and scale.

Add shoes.

Sketch in the pedals.

Add the handlebars using the construction lines as a guide.

Add the main frame of the bike using straight lines.

Finish the detail of the head, hat, and hair.

Add detail and creases to the pants, especially behind the knee.

Add dark tone to areas where light would not reach.

Add detail to the shoes.

Finish the dark metal handlebars.

Finish the frame of the bike, adding a chain and details to the pedals. Add tone to suggest metal tubes.

Complete the wheels, adding dark tone for the rubber tires and lines for the spokes.

Remove any unwanted construction lines.

17

Skysurfing

Skysurfing is a high-altitude extreme sport. A skysurfer freefalls from an airplane with a board attached to his feet, surfing the air and performing stunts on the way to the ground.

Start by sketching in a simple stick figure with dots for the joints.

Draw ovals for the head, body, hips, and hands.

Draw the shape of the hands.

Draw simple tube shapes for the arms. Add circles for the elbows.

Position basic facial features and add a neck.

Connect the body and hip ovals together.

Sketch in tube shapes for the legs and attach them to the hip oval.

This arm and hand are shortened because of perspective.

Add circles for the knees.

Sketch in the board.

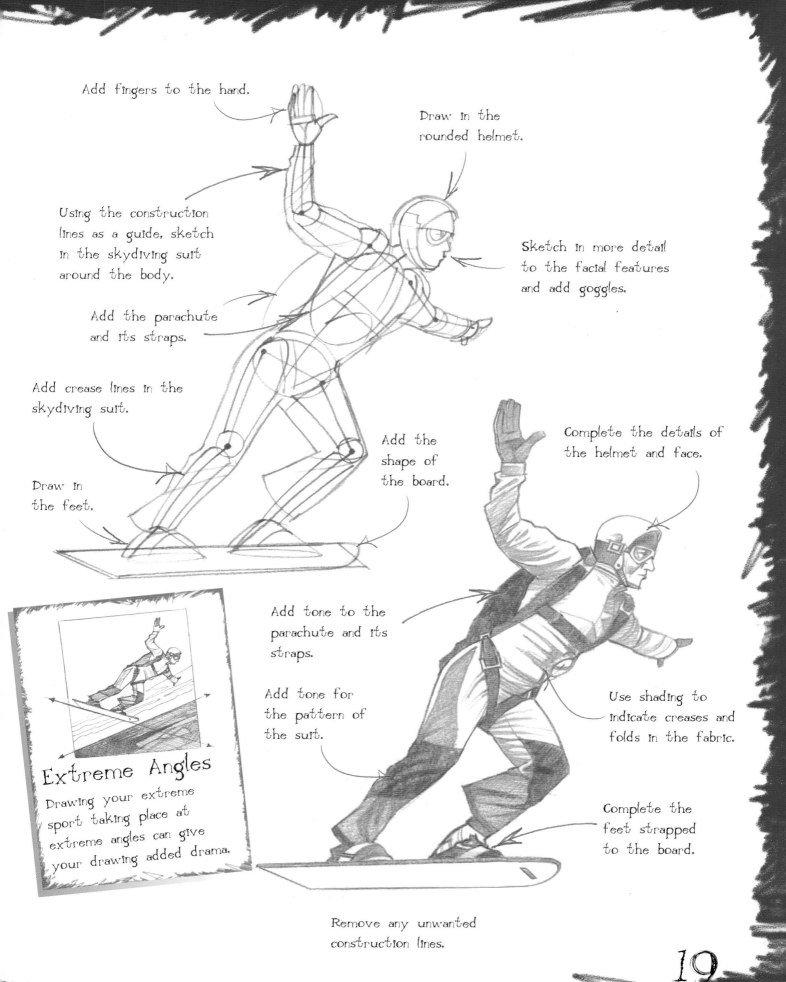

Add fingers to the hand.

Draw in the rounded helmet.

Using the construction lines as a guide, sketch in the skydiving suit around the body.

Sketch in more detail to the facial features and add goggles.

Add the parachute and its straps.

Add crease lines in the skydiving suit.

Add the shape of the board.

Complete the details of the helmet and face.

Draw in the feet.

Add tone to the parachute and its straps.

Add tone for the pattern of the suit.

Use shading to indicate creases and folds in the fabric.

Extreme Angles

Drawing your extreme sport taking place at extreme angles can give your drawing added drama.

Complete the feet strapped to the board.

Remove any unwanted construction lines.

19

ATV Racing

These powerful quad bikes are adapted to be fast, lightweight, and maneuverable for many different types of racing. "ATV" stands for "all terrain vehicle."

Sketch in a simple seated stick figure with dots for the joints.

Draw two straight lines to position the front and rear wheels.

Sketch in the main chassis of the ATV.

Add the shape of the wheels (see page 12).

Using the construction lines as a guide, draw in tube-shaped arms and legs, adding circles at the knees and elbows.

Sketch in some facial features.

Add detail to the main chassis of the ATV.

Define the shape of the wheels.

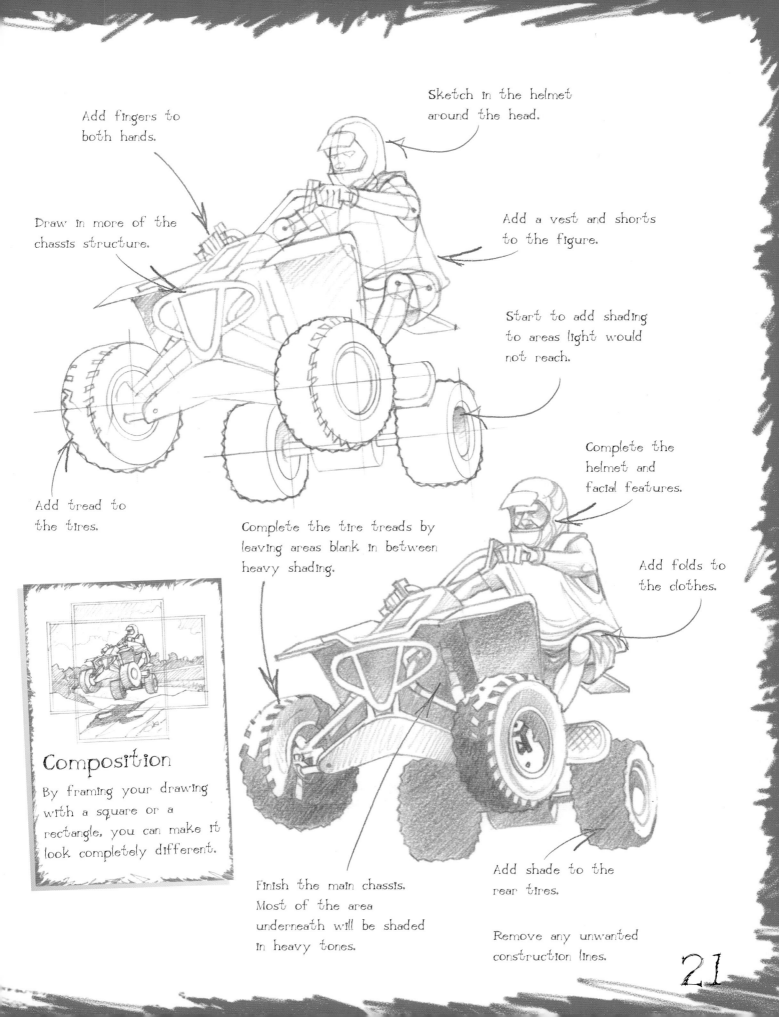

Sketch in the helmet around the head.

Add fingers to both hands.

Draw in more of the chassis structure.

Add a vest and shorts to the figure.

Start to add shading to areas light would not reach.

Add tread to the tires.

Complete the helmet and facial features.

Complete the tire treads by leaving areas blank in between heavy shading.

Add folds to the clothes.

Composition

By framing your drawing with a square or a rectangle, you can make it look completely different.

Finish the main chassis. Most of the area underneath will be shaded in heavy tones.

Add shade to the rear tires.

Remove any unwanted construction lines.

21

Wakeboarding

This extreme water sport involves being towed behind a boat at high speeds on a small wakeboard. Hitting the wake of the boat enables the wakeboarder to fly into the air and perform amazing tricks.

Draw ovals for the head, body, and hands.

Add a line for the tow-rope handle.

Start by sketching in a simple stick figure with dots for the joints.

Add the shape of the feet.

Add some facial details.

Sketch in simple tube shapes for the arms.

Add circles for the elbows.

Draw two parallel lines for the wakeboard.

Draw the hand shapes.

Add more shape to the feet.

Draw simple tube shapes for the legs, adding circles for the knees.

Add curved, windswept lines for hair.

Using the construction lines as a guide, add the curved shape of the arms.

Sketch in the tow rope.

Add fingers to the hands.

Draw a vest on the figure.

Draw a basic boot shape around the feet.

Add long, baggy shorts.

Add tone to define muscle structure.

Finish the details of the tow rope and handle.

Complete the details of the head and hair.

Complete the shorts with a graphic design and creases.

Add folds and creases to the vest.

Finish the boot details.

Add the waves and splash of water.

Complete the wakeboard.

Remove any unwanted construction lines.

23

Skateboarding

One of the most popular extreme sports is skateboarding. Skateboarders have terrific balance and can achieve many spectacular tricks and stunts.

Start by sketching in a simple stick figure with dots for the joints.

Draw ovals for the head, body, hips, and hands.

Add a straight line with a slight curve at one end for the deck of the skateboard.

Add some facial features.

Draw in the shape of the hands.

Add circles for the knees.

Sketch in simple tube shapes for the arms and legs.

Add the shape of the feet.

Draw tube shapes for the skateboard wheels.

Sketch in the shape of the feet.

Draw the fingers.

Add a cap to the head.

Draw both arms using the construction lines as a guide. This arm is very foreshortened because of its angle.

Sketch in the trousers.

Add a vest.

Separate the tube into individual wheels.

Add muscle detail to the arms.

Complete the facial details.

Start to draw the skateboarder's shoes.

Add dark tone to areas where light would not reach.

Add creases to the pants fabric.

Finish drawing the skateboard.

Shadows

Adding a shadow to your drawing can give it added drama. The shape of the skater's shadow will depend on the direction of the light source.

Finish drawing the skateboard shoes, adding laces and detail.

Remove any unwanted construction lines.

Skydiving

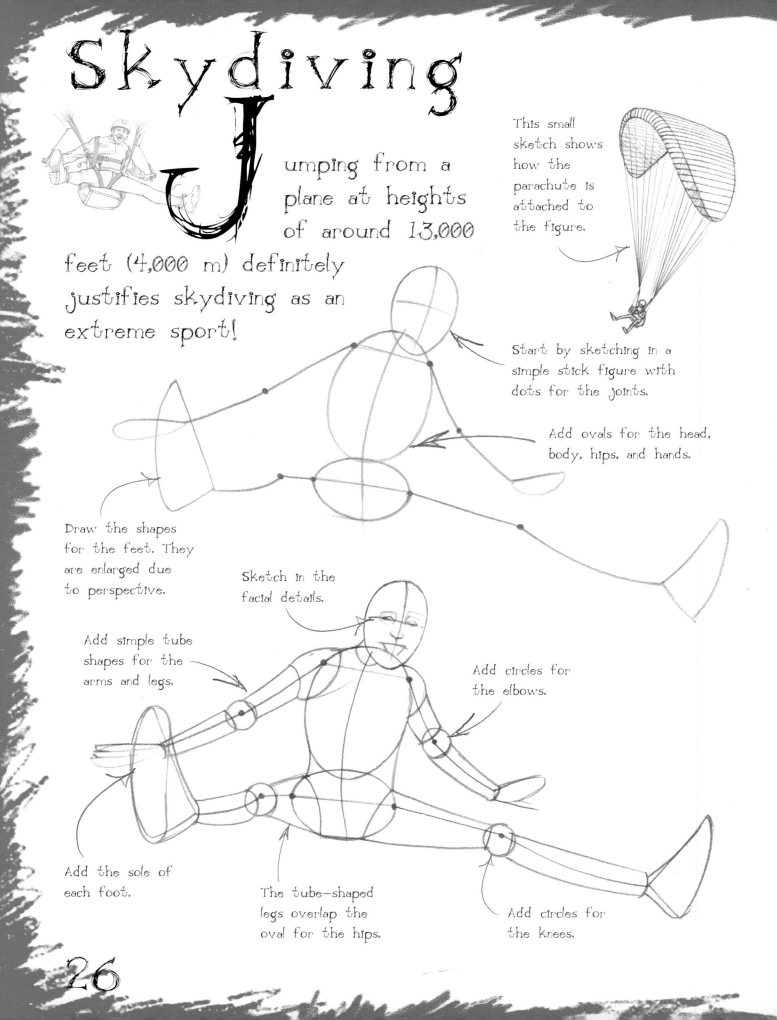

Jumping from a plane at heights of around 13,000 feet (4,000 m) definitely justifies skydiving as an extreme sport!

This small sketch shows how the parachute is attached to the figure.

Start by sketching in a simple stick figure with dots for the joints.

Add ovals for the head, body, hips, and hands.

Draw the shapes for the feet. They are enlarged due to perspective.

Sketch in the facial details.

Add simple tube shapes for the arms and legs.

Add circles for the elbows.

Add the sole of each foot.

The tube-shaped legs overlap the oval for the hips.

Add circles for the knees.

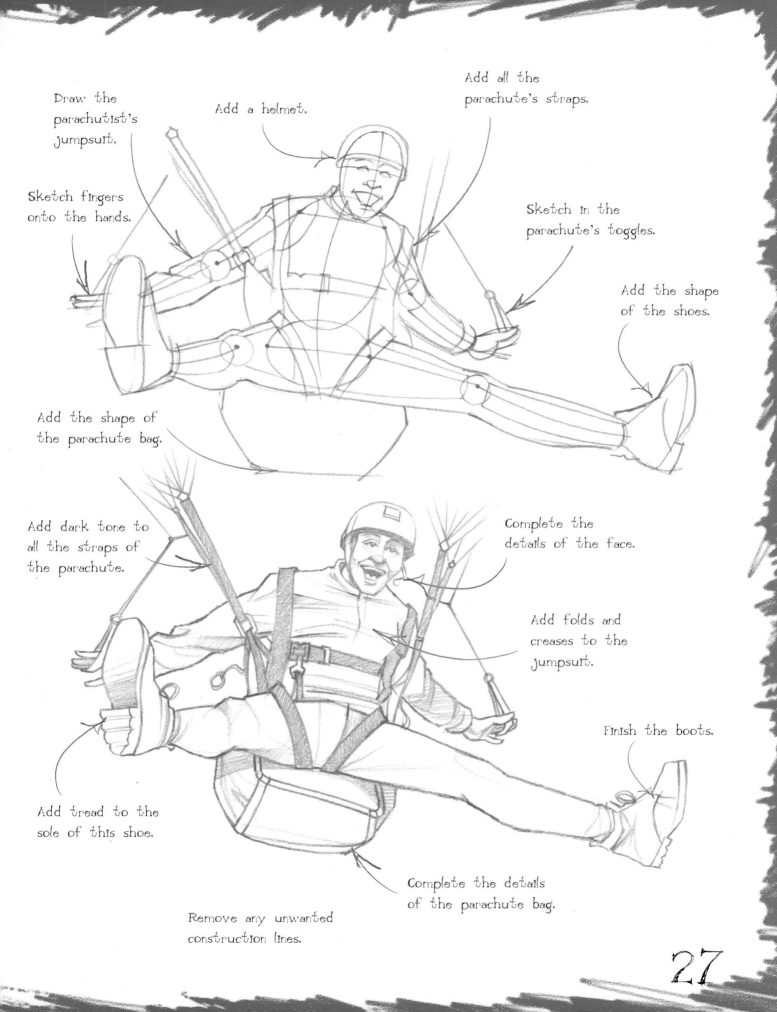

Draw the parachutist's jumpsuit.

Add a helmet.

Add all the parachute's straps.

Sketch fingers onto the hands.

Sketch in the parachute's toggles.

Add the shape of the shoes.

Add the shape of the parachute bag.

Add dark tone to all the straps of the parachute.

Complete the details of the face.

Add folds and creases to the jumpsuit.

Finish the boots.

Add tread to the sole of this shoe.

Complete the details of the parachute bag.

Remove any unwanted construction lines.

27

River Rafting

River rafting is an extreme water sport. Each team will try to successfully navigate a rubber raft down fast-flowing rivers and through rapids.

Sketch in five seated stick figures with dots for the joints.

Draw ovals for the heads, bodies, and hands of all five figures.

Draw a line between each figure's hands for the paddle handles.

Sketch in some curved lines to position the raft.

Add simple tube-shaped arms for each figure.

Add circles for the elbows and knees.

Add the blades of the paddles.

Sketch in more of the upper raft using curved lines.

Draw simple tube-shaped legs.

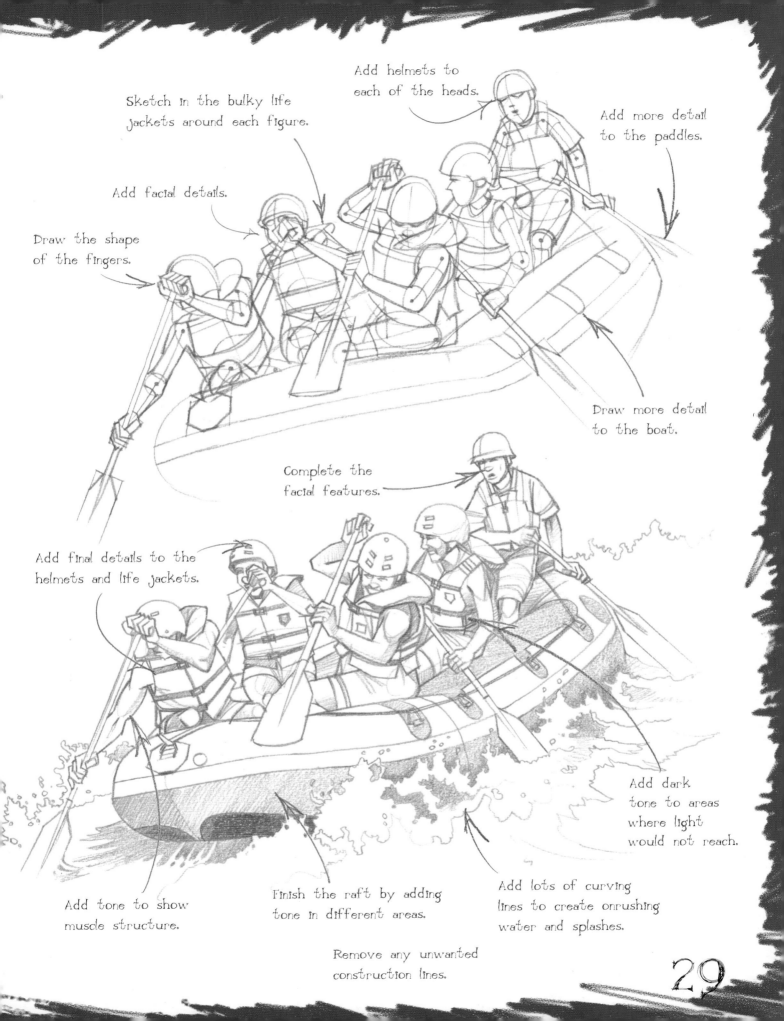

Add helmets to
each of the heads.

Sketch in the bulky life
jackets around each figure.

Add more detail
to the paddles.

Add facial details.

Draw the shape
of the fingers.

Draw more detail
to the boat.

Complete the
facial features.

Add final details to the
helmets and life jackets.

Add dark
tone to areas
where light
would not reach.

Add tone to show
muscle structure.

Finish the raft by adding
tone in different areas.

Add lots of curving
lines to create onrushing
water and splashes.

Remove any unwanted
construction lines.

Kitesurfing

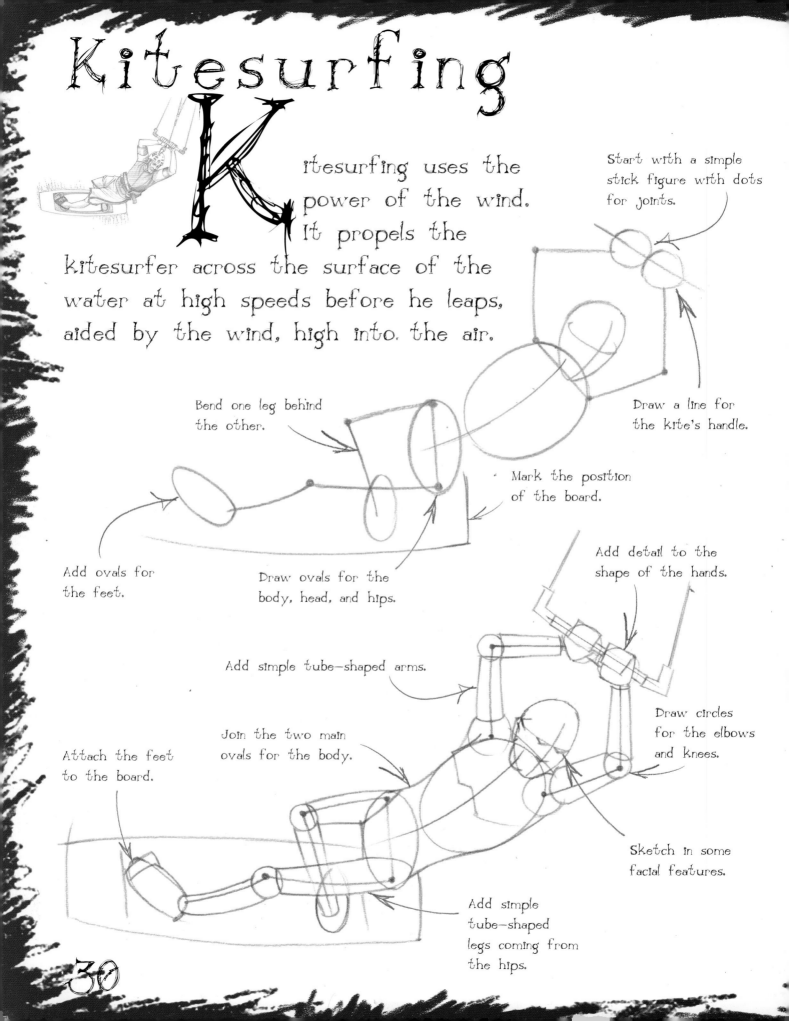

Kitesurfing uses the power of the wind. It propels the kitesurfer across the surface of the water at high speeds before he leaps, aided by the wind, high into the air.

Start with a simple stick figure with dots for joints.

Draw a line for the kite's handle.

Bend one leg behind the other.

Mark the position of the board.

Add ovals for the feet.

Draw ovals for the body, head, and hips.

Add detail to the shape of the hands.

Add simple tube-shaped arms.

Draw circles for the elbows and knees.

Join the two main ovals for the body.

Attach the feet to the board.

Sketch in some facial features.

Add simple tube-shaped legs coming from the hips.

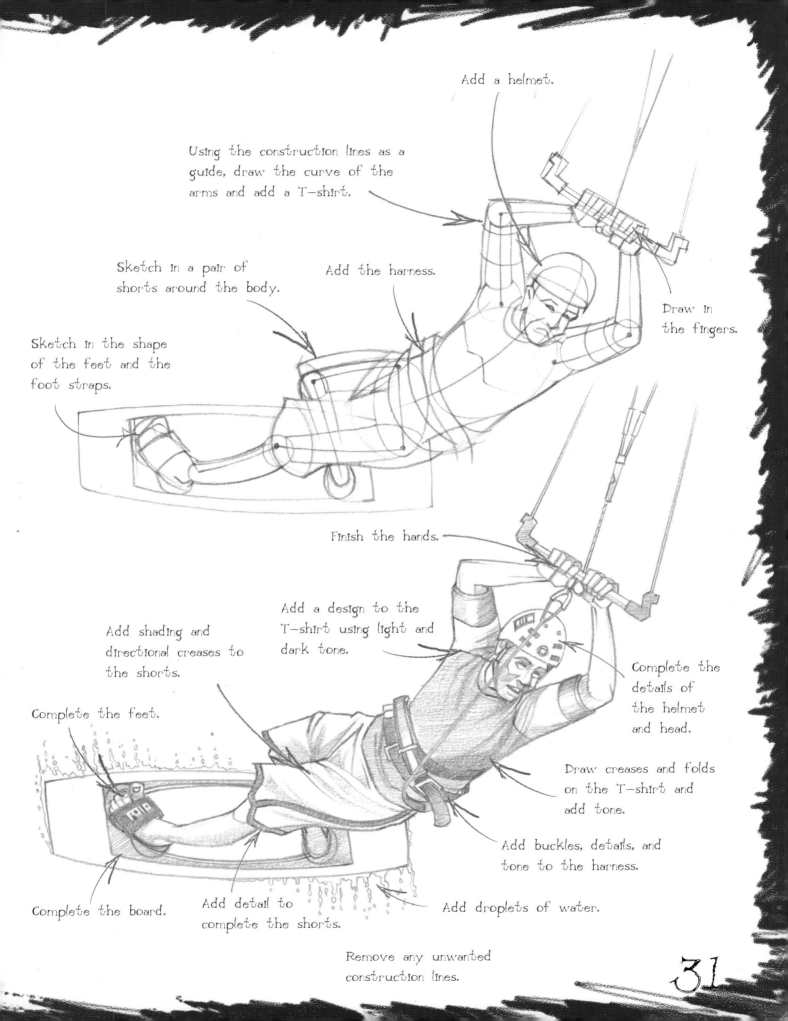

Add a helmet.

Using the construction lines as a guide, draw the curve of the arms and add a T-shirt.

Draw in the fingers.

Sketch in a pair of shorts around the body.

Add the harness.

Sketch in the shape of the feet and the foot straps.

Finish the hands.

Add a design to the T-shirt using light and dark tone.

Complete the details of the helmet and head.

Add shading and directional creases to the shorts.

Complete the feet.

Draw creases and folds on the T-shirt and add tone.

Complete the board.

Add detail to complete the shorts.

Add buckles, details, and tone to the harness.

Add droplets of water.

Remove any unwanted construction lines.

31

Glossary

composition (kom-puh-ZIH-shun) The positioning of a picture on the drawing paper.

construction lines (kun-STRUK-shun LYNZ) Guidelines used in the early stages of a drawing, which are usually erased.

cross-hatching (KRAWS-hach-ing) A series of criss-crossing lines used to add shade to a drawing.

fixative (FIK-suh-tiv) A type of resin that is sprayed over a finished drawing to prevent smudging. It should only be used by an adult.

hatching (HACH-ing) A series of parallel lines used to add shade to a drawing.

light source (LYT SORS) The direction from which the light seems to come in a drawing.

silhouette (sih-luh-WET) A drawing that shows only a dark shape, like a shadow.

sketchbook (SKECH-buk) A book in which sketches are made.

three-dimensional (three-deh-MENCH-nul) Having an effect of depth, so as to look lifelike or real.

vanishing point (VA-nish-ing POYNT) The place in a perspective drawing where parallel lines appear to meet.

Index

Web Sites

Due to the changing nature of Internet links, PowerKids Press has developed an online list of Web sites related to the subject of this book. This site is updated regularly. Please use this link to access the list:

www.powerkidslinks.com/htd/exsports/